D0897668

# Collected Poems 1944-1979

Kingsley Amis

Hutchinson of London

Hutchinson & Co. (Publishers) Ltd
3 Fitzroy Square, London W1P 6JD

London Melbourne Sydney Auckland
Wellington Johannesburg and agencies
throughout the world

First published 1979
© Kingsley Amis 1979

Set in VIP Bembo Roman

Printed in Great Britain by
The Anchor Press Ltd and bound by
Wm Brendon & Son Ltd,
both of Tiptree, Essex

British Library CIP data
Amis, Kingsley
    Collected poems, 1944–1979.
    I. Title
    821'.9'14          PR6001.M6A17

ISBN 0 09 136790 5

To John Betjeman
and in memory of our friend
John Allison

# Contents

# Author's Note

With a few exceptions in the interest of tidiness, the poems here are arranged chronologically in the order in which (to the best of my recollection) I started work on each. Most of them are reprinted from earlier collections of mine, as follows:

The first six poems from *Bright November*, Fortune Press, 1947

The next forty-two ('Legends' to 'Romance' inclusive) from *A Case of Samples*, Victor Gollancz Ltd, 1956

The next thirty-six ('An Ever-Fixed Mark' to 'Aberdarcy: the Chaucer Road' inclusive) from *A Look Found the Estate*, Jonathan Cape Ltd, 1967

The final twenty ('South' and the rest) have not been collected before. My acknowledgements are made to the editors respectively of *Encounter*, *The London Magazine*, the *New Statesman*, The *Observer*, *Poetry Nation* and the *Spectator*, in one or other of which they were first printed. 'Wasted' first appeared with the Poem of the Month Club.

# Collected Poems 1944-1979

# Letter to Elisabeth

Even the perfect year must finish, love,
Just as the winter we found hard to leave.
Though all we knew was cold and never private
Not the disguise of summer shall disprove it;
In public rooms we guessed at silence, and
Discussed the end of what has had no end.
Where none would pause we found an hour to wait
And clung together when the streets were wet.
Now in a parted meanwhile rings the beat
Of married hearts; my scene has shifted, but
Still flows your northern river like a pulse,
Carrying blood to bodies at the poles.
The jealous stranger has no power to harm
A year that brings us always nearer home.
We wait only until the clock sees fit
To call our morning; there shall be no fate
To colour our departure with more years.
There shall be no more No nor no more Yes,
No need for speech or thought. A time for feeling,
Uniting lovers in the spring, fulfilling
The fumbling gesture and the hoarded pain,
The static hand of love wrenching the pen,
Shall come to us in our new year, shall come
As certainly as separation came;
Know then the pride of being not too late,
Of bringing every look into the light;
At last, love, love has taught me to speak straight,
To make my body walk without a strut;
Dearest, on our first anniversary
Nothing exists now that can go awry.
The eyes that looked good-bye will look at love
As from this sleep we know ourselves alive.

# Radar

Kolster and Dunmore made a remarkable valve
Which would bind forever the sense of the plunging
    wave;
Riddling the grid they gazed at a colander
Bending like a bough to and fro in the created heat.

Never was a glass cage seen like theirs;
The throttled note pushing unasked into the ear
Cancelled humanity, forced the hand to move,
Crammed quivering gauges with eyes that never
    closed.

Meanwhile the radiation sprang from the tentative
    rod,
Adored by the hymn of the mains singing like ladies
Countries away from the white laboratory's quiet,
Sped by the sea to the sky's alphabetical layers.

Like a sunbeam the wave-train smote the metal
    mirror,
The wing of the monoplane at its English ceiling,
And with deathless energy stooped at its home and
    maker;
A sign fallen from heaven for the waiting guns.

And so the screaming electrode in Kolster's house
Was in labour, you see, with the crude mechanical
    wind
That blew through Dunmore, making of the
    innocent scientist
A living directing-horn for the ears of war.

On the enemy side stood aerials like the bereaved
Who mask their essence with respectable sound;
And Kolster and Dunmore heard their interference,
But it was dismissed for them as a stray effect.

# Belgian Winter

The plains awkwardly revealed by history,
War in the wrong place, the usual day,
Stupid in the dignity of shot,
Blunt the ambitions, make all speak alone.
Martyrdom is a thing of cities, not
The country of the dull; the beautiful
And eloquent showily marked for death;
Unmoving faces are destined to live long.

From my window stretches the earth, containing
  wrecks:
The burrowing tank, the flat grave, the
Lorry with underside showing, like a dead rabbit.
The trees that smear all light into a mess;
World of one tone, stolid with fallen snow.
Here is the opaque ice, the hum-drum winter,
The splintered houses suddenly come upon
Left over from wounds that pierced a different
  people.

But there are people here, unable to understand,
Randy for cigarettes, moving hands too
Jerky to move in love; their women matrons, their
  daughters
Fanatically guarded or whores with lovely teeth;
The sons come from somewhere else, fair of skin;
The children have thick white socks and an English
  laugh,
Bearers of flowers, quiet and pointlessly clean,
Showing their parents up, not easily amused.

Behind is the city, a garnished London, a Paris
That has no idea how to live, of Chirico squares;
A feast of enemies, the stranger entertained
With opera and lesbian exhibitions,
Assurances of enjoyment and sameness; the pubs
Like railway buffets, bare and impersonal.
Smiles exclude the hypothesis of starving, but
The conqueror is advised to keep to the boulevards.

Then if history had a choice, he would point his
   cameras
Oh yes anywhere but here, any time but now;
But this is given us as the end of something
Important, something we must try to remember;
No music or kisses we want attend the fade-out,
Only a same sky or an embarrassing room,
Lust for something and a lust for no one,
Aloneness of crowds, infidelity, love's torture.

# Beowulf

So, bored with dragons, he lay down to sleep,
Locking for good his massive hoard of words
(Discuss and illustrate), forgetting now
The hope of heathens, muddled thoughts on fate.

Councils would have to get along without him:
The peerless prince had taken his last bribe
(*Lif is læne*); useless now the byrnie
Hard and hand-locked, fit for a baseball catcher.

Only with Grendel was he man-to-man;
Grendel's dam was his only sort of woman
(Weak conjugation). After they were gone
How could he stand the bench-din, the yelp-word?

Someone has told us this man was a hero.
Must we then reproduce his paradigms,
Trace out his rambling regress to his forbears
(An instance of Old English harking-back)?

# Bed and Breakfast

Sometimes a parting leaves only a room
That frames a void in yellow wallpapers,
Unpersoned by such brief indifferent use;
But love, once broken off, builds a response
In the final turning pause that sees nothing
Is left, and grieves though nothing happened here.

So, stranger, when you come here to unpack,
To look like me excited on the garden,
Expect from me nothing but a false wish
That, going, you ignore all other partings,
And find no ghosts that growl or whinny of
Kisses from nowhere, negligible tears.

# Retrospect

Our untouched photograph of years seems new
As if because of what we have not done;
Our dreams no longer qualify us for
Returns to feeling or a life begun;

For life, too feminine, always insists
On smiling when we want to be serious,
Has no sense of the cinema; and forked
By the black knight of living, we must lose

Our eyes or our invisible empire,
And it is his move. So loudspeakers boom
Departure's practised accents, and my room
Shudders with candles and voices that fail,

Refusing tears to circumstance. When hands
Link that do not mean to hold on for ever,
Their touch is cold, is cold that silence ends
And love is always moving somewhere else.

# Legends

Sleepy, the nurse forgot the end of the story,
And offered a plausible fantasy instead;
So the young rider, weakened by age she added,
Lost his message and went adrift for good,
Turning off the highroad of history
To wander without hope in fabled night.
Deceived like this, children in their dreams
Set food before the tent of him who led
Their fathers into ambush. And through the house
The ghost must walk where none remembers his
    name,
And see nothing he knows in his childhood's room.

Age, then, blurs all; whose age it does not matter,
For any years will curl the ivy over
The windows behind which nothing happens yet,
And, even without the sun, the rain will fall
To write in stone a deepening signature,
While far from sight water grows in the well.
The mean becomes the cherished, if it remains.

A new age, perhaps, will change our cruelty
Into the quaint naughtiness of romance,
Its dismal end always put off till to-morrow;
Someone may excuse the works we have reared,
Read charm in error, as an ancient fresco
Pardons the hand that fashioned it and murder;
Some ghost of ours may stop, and from his window
With dead eyes watch the death of the last gun,
The grasp of power as feeble as his own.

# Lessons

How long, when hand of master is withdrawn,
Will hand of pupil move as if it stayed?
The books once closed, the classroom blind run
    down,
Who thinks of lessons now there is no need?

Docility, of feature or of mind,
Is glad to wither when the tongue is free;
Even if one phrase, one shared thought, remained,
Ten more will come and go by half-past four.

Therefore let all who teach discard this pride,
That anything is learnt except to please;
When fingers touch, or how love's names are said,
Like any lessons, change with time and place;

So here and now, with individual care,
This one sole way hand may be laid on hand,
Voice only with one voice may learn to cry,
And thus tongue lie with tongue, thus mind with
    mind.

But out of school, all ways the hand will move,
Forget the private hour, and touch the world;
The voice will bawl, slur the accent of love,
The tongue slop sweets, the mind lounge home
    expelled.

# Masters

That horse whose rider fears to jump will fall,
Riflemen miss if orders sound unsure;
They only are secure who seem secure;
    Who lose their voice, lose all.

Those whom heredity or guns have made
Masters, must show it by a common speech;
Expected words in the same tone from each
    Will always be obeyed.

Likewise with stance, with gestures, and with face;
No more than mouth need move when words are
      said,
No more than hand to strike, or point ahead;
    Like slaves, limbs learn their place.

In triumph as in mutiny unmoved,
These make their public act their private good,
Their words in lounge or courtroom understood,
    But themselves never loved.

The eyes that will not look, the twitching cheek,
The hands that sketch what mouth would fear to
      own,
Only these make us known, and we are known
    Only as we are weak:

By yielding mastery the will is freed,
For it is by surrender that we live,
And we are taken if we wish to give,
    Are needed if we need.

# The Last War

The first country to die was normal in the evening,
Ate a good but plain dinner, chatted with some
        friends
Over a glass, and went to bed soon after ten;
And in the morning was found disfigured and dead.
      That was a lucky one.

At breakfast the others heard about it, and kept
Their eyes on their plates. Who was guilty? No one
      knew,
But by lunch-time three more would never eat
      again.
The rest appealed for frankness, quietly cocked their
      guns,
      Declared "This can't go on".

They were right. Only the strongest turned up for
      tea:
The old ones with the big estates hadn't survived
The slobbering blindfold violence of the afternoon.
One killer or many? Was it a gang, or all-against-all?
      Somebody must have known.

But each of them sat there watching the others, until
Night came and found them anxious to get it over.
Then the lights went out. A few might have lived,
      even then;
Innocent, they thought (at first) it still mattered
      what
      You had or hadn't done.

They were wrong. One had been lenient with his
        servants;
Another ran an island brothel, but rarely left it;
The third owned a museum, the fourth a remarkable
        gun;
The name of a fifth was quite unknown, but in the
        end
        What was the difference? None.

Homicide, pacifist, crusader, tyrant, adventurer,
        boor
Staggered about moaning, shooting into the dark.
Next day, to tidy up as usual, the sun came in
When they and their ammunition were all finished,
        And found himself alone.

Upset, he looked them over, to separate, if he could,
The assassins from the victims, but every face
Had taken on the flat anonymity of pain;
And soon they'll all smell alike, he thought, and felt
        sick,
        And went to bed at noon.

# Dirty Story

Twice daily, at noon and dusk, if we are lucky,
We hear fresh news of you, an oral cutting
From your unlimited biography.

To-day a butcher, you cuckolded the grocer,
Fouling his sugar, in thirty seconds only,
All the while tickling a pretty customer;

Yesterday you posed as a winking parson
Or a gull from the north, cloaking your
    belly-laughter
With a false voice that mourned for what you'd
    done;

To-morrow, in what shrines gaily excreting,
Will you, our champion even if defeated,
Bring down a solemn edifice with one swing?

Hero of single action, epic expert,
Beggar prince and bandit chief of the sexy,
Spry Juan, lifter of the lifted skirt,

What is the secret of your howling successes—
Your tongue never tardy with the punch sentence,
Your you-know-what in fabulous readiness?

Is it no more than the researcher's patience
To ransack life's laboratory, and labour
Ten years distilling salts to be used once;

To nose out the precisely suitable landscape,
The curiously jealous, the uniquely randy,
Then blow them all up in a riposte or rape?

If so, your exploits should be read in silence,
Words bred of such travail move none to smiling,
But all to an uneasy reverence:

Reverence at such will to live in stories;
Uneasy, because we see behind your glories
Our own nasty defeats, nastier victories.

# The Real Earth

She smiled when, put to bed at twilight,
   She saw the quilt prepare for night;
Guarding the sheep of fluff that lay
   In channelled fields, sewn squares by day,
She paced her pillow's neighbourhood,
   Its lace a frozen wood.

Grown up, she thought the earth a cover
   To pull up to the chin; to her
All scenes were blankets for her bed,
   Homely with warmth; all roads that led
Through rumpled fields to any town
   Seams on an eiderdown.

In her great bed one night, she trembled,
   And thought what covered her seemed cold,
Every moment more like the ground.
   Too drowsy now for fear, she found
Softly upflowing from her feet
   An unaired, a soiled sheet.

# Alternatives

It starts: a white girl in a dark house
Alone with the piano, playing a short song;
Lilies and silk stand quiet, silent the street,
The oil-lamp void of flame. Her long dress
Is rigid at the hem when her arms move
To hush, not urge, the current of the notes.

Below in a red light stoops the murderer,
Black in the cellar among straw and glass.
Dust cracks under his feet, his finger scrapes
The limed wall, then the bottom stair's edge,
And soon the wooden door creaks and yawns;
He shuffles towards the music. It ends.

Let bewilderment tie his hands, I cry,
Some flower in the wallpaper bind his brain,
So that the girl's room never fills with him
And the song never ends, I never hear
The jangling as her body falls awry
And the black lid shuts on her clenched hands.

But something says: Neither or both for you;
The house always empty, or this end.
Or would you rather she smiled as she played,
Hearing a step she knows, and sitting still,
Waited for the hands to move, not round
Her throat, but to her eager breasts?

# Wrong Words

Half-shut, our eye dawdles down the page
Seeing the word love, the word death, the word life,
Rhyme-words of poets in a silver age:
Silver of the bauble, not of the knife.

Too fluent, drenching with confectionery
One image, one event's hard outline,
The words of failure's voluptuary
Descant around love—love of a routine.

There follow high words from a thwarted child
Rightly denied what it would foul, threatening
Grown-ups with its death, eager to gild
The pose of writhing with the pose of resigning.

But loneliness, the word never said,
Pleads to be recognised through their conceits;
Behind their frantic distortion lies the dread,
Unforced, unblurred, of real defeats:

Their real ladies would not follow the book,
Wrong ladies, happy with wrong words, wrong
    lives;
Careening now, they blazed, while none would
    look,
  The distress signals of their superlatives.

# A Dream of Fair Women

The door still swinging to, and girls revive,
Aeronauts in the utmost altitudes
　　Of boredom fainting, dive
Into the bright oxygen of my nod;
Angels as well, a squadron of draped nudes,
　　They roar towards their god.

Militant all, they fight to take my hat,
No more as yet; the other men retire
　　Insulted, gestured at;
Each girl presses on me her share of what
Makes up the barn-door target of desire:
　　And I am a crack shot.

Speech fails them, amorous, but each one's look,
Endorsed in other ways, begs me to sign
　　Her body's autograph-book;
"Me first, Kingsley; I'm cleverest" each declares,
But no gourmet races downstairs to dine,
　　Nor will I race upstairs.

Feigning aplomb, perhaps for half an hour,
I hover, and am shown by each princess
　　The entrance to her tower;
Open, in that its tenant throws the key
At once to anyone, but not unless
　　The anyone is me.

Now from the corridor their fathers cheer,
Their brothers, their young men; the cheers increase
　　As soon as I appear;
From each I win a handshake and sincere
Congratulations; from the chief of police
　　A nod, a wink, a leer.

This over, all delay is over too;
The first eight girls (the roster now agreed)
  Leap on me, and undo . . .
But honesty impels me to confess
That this is "all a dream", which was, indeed,
  Not difficult to guess.

But wait; not "just a dream", because, though good
And beautiful, it is also true, and hence
  Is rarely understood;
Who would choose any workable ideal
In here and now's giant circumference,
  If that small room were real?

Only the best; the others find, have found
Love's ordinary distances too great,
  And, eager, stand their ground;
Map-drunk explorers, dry-land sailors, they
See no arrival that can compensate
  For boredom on the way;

And, seeming doctrinaire, but really weak,
Limelighted dolls guttering in their brain,
  They come with me, to seek
The halls of theoretical delight,
The women of that ever-fresh terrain,
  The night after tonight.

# The Silent Room

In his low-ceilinged oaken room
The corpse finds pastimes of the tomb
   Cramped into scratching nose
   And counting fingers, toes.

Fed up with cackling folderols,
He longs for books, a wireless, dolls,
   Anything that might keep
   His dusty eyes from sleep.

For sleep would bring too-accurate
Dreams of the heavenly garden-fête
   Where the immortals walk,
   Pledged to immortal talk.

Dazed by respect or laughter, he
Would reel from saw to repartee,
   Ecstatic for the first
   Five thousand hours, at worst.

Verbal set-pieces yet would blaze,
And rocket-patterns yet amaze
   For twice as long, to draw
   His eye, not now his awe;

Then to one glow the varied fire
Would sink, the breezy bangs expire
   In mutters, and the bare
   Sticks char in the bright air.

The walkers on the endless lawn
Talk but to hide an endless yawn,
 Stale in the mouth of each
 An old, unwanted speech.

Foreseeing then a second sleep
(Of unknown dreams), the corpse must keep
 Permanently awake,
 And wait for an earthquake.

Earthquakes are few, brief their effect.
But wood soon rots: he can expect
 A far less rare relief
 From boredom, and less brief;

At last, maddened but merry, he
Finds never-tiring company:
 Slug, with foul rhymes to tell;
 Worm, with small-talk from hell.

# Against Romanticism

A traveller who walks a temperate zone
   —Woods devoid of beasts, roads that please the
     foot—
Finds that its decent surface grows too thin:
   Something unperceived fumbles at his nerves.
To please an ingrown taste for anarchy
   Torrid images circle in the wood,
And sweat for recognition up the road,
   Cramming close the air with their bookish cries.
All senses then are glad to gasp: the eye
   Smeared with garish paints, tickled up with
     ghosts
That brandish warnings or an abstract noun;
   Melodies from shards, memories from coal,
Or saws from powdered tombstones thump the ear;
   Bodies rich with heat wriggle to the touch,
And verbal scents made real spellbind the nose;
   Incense, frankincense; legendary the taste
Of drinks or fruits or tongues laid on the tongue.
   Over all, a grand meaning fills the scene,
And sets the brain raging with prophecy,
   Raging to discard real time and place,
Raging to build a better time and place
   Than the ones which give prophecy its field
To work, the calm material for its rage,
   And the context which makes it prophecy.

Better, of course, if images were plain,
   Warnings clearly said, shapes put down quite still
Within the fingers' reach, or else nowhere;
   But complexities crowd the simplest thing,
And flaw the surface that they cannot break.

Let us make at least visions that we need:
Let mine be pallid, so that it cannot
   Force a single glance, form a single word;
An afternoon long-drawn and silent, with
   Buildings free from all grime of history,
The people total strangers, the grass cut,
   Not long, voluble swooning wilderness,
And green, not parched or soured by frantic suns
   Doubling the commands of a rout of gods,
Nor trampled by the drivelling unicorn;
   Let the sky be clean of officious birds
Punctiliously flying on the left;
   Let there be a path leading out of sight,
And at its other end a temperate zone:
   Woods devoid of beasts, roads that please the
      foot.

# Departure

For one month afterwards the eye stays true,
And sees the other's face held still and free
Of ornament; then tires of peering down
A narrow vista, and the month runs out.

Too young, this eye will claim the merit of
A faithful sentry frozen at his post
And not a movement seen; yet ranges over
Far other tracts, its object lost, corrupt.

Nor should I now swell to halloo the names
Of feelings that no one needs to remember,
Nor caper with my posy of wilted avowals
To clutter up your path I should wish clear.

Perhaps it is not too late to crane the eye
And find you, distant and small, but as you are;
Otherwise I will keep you honestly blurred,
Not a bland refraction of sweet mirrors.

# Swansea Bay

Maps look impressive; to be anywhere
In villages rich with conventional signs,
Knowing that things ten miles away are there,
Seems happiness; roads fenced by dotted lines
Must run between pictorial solitudes;
Waters deserve their blue of remote, still,
And best at evening; and enamelled green
Becomes a phrase again, furnishing woods
With billiard-table moss, baize-apron leaves.
All must run for once to our own will,
Be and enact our need, and none believes
That any sour notes hide in a scored scene.

The far side of this bay is like a map:
Something small denotes a tower, a steeple,
Shading points out the contoured slopes, a scrap
Of smoke is houses, and movement movement of
    people.
They are the chance effect, the frontal mess
Against the background's paper authority;
However trite, some kind of recognition
—Immodesties of love or weariness—
Has got to make their presence relevance,
To see in a blank field an absent city;
People must enter the eye's lonely dance,
Or leave it reeling at its blind vision:

# On Staying Still

Half-way down the beach
A broken boat lies;
Black in every light,
But swathed with sand that glows
From black to chocolate
Then ginger-dust. The seas
Soak it for no reason
Each tide-rise, finding it
Dried by the sun for no
Reason, or already wet
With rain before they are near
To strike poses of passion:
Bravery of blind colour,
Noble gesture of spray,
And eloquence of loud noise
That shake not a single spar.
The hulk's only use
Is as mark for pebble-thrower
Or shade for small anemone,
But that is not nothing;
And staying still is more,
When all else is moving
To no end, whether
Or not choice is free.
Good that decay recalls
(By being slow and steady)
Blossom, fruitful change
Of tree to coal, not any
Changeless tidal fury.

# Nerves

The sun sinks behind houses, much too early;
Its warmth leaves stone and flesh, and the body
  Drowses, and safe in the dark
The nerves creep out, much too quickly.

They breed heat, no warmth, by their own
    writhing;
Their tremor is the tremor of the unwilling
  Hand, which to steady itself
Must touch somebody or something.

They twitch the head down in mock approval,
Mock humility, mock self-acquittal;
  They make the will an ant
Scuttling about its chalked circle.

For outlet, give me a fourth dimension;
For health, seal off this moist possession
  Behind sterilised flesh;
Sear it with a vast midday's iron,

Before some winter solstice lets it run
Through the small day to build its furred cocoon
  From head to foot, unbroken
Between me and air, movement, the sun.

# The End

The mirror holds: small common objects fill
Its eye impatient, sore with keeping still.
   The book, the person stupefy,
   Merely because they fill its eye.

The mirror breaks, and fragments wheel and flare
—Before their mercury dissolves in air—
   To seize the person for one look,
   To catch one image of the book.

# The Value of Suffering

Surrounded for years with all the most assured
Tokens of size and sense—the broad thick table
Triple-banked with food, too much to eat, and
    flowers
Too mixed and many to smell, and ladies too
Ready, sating ambition before it formed—
He went on hunting in the right costume,
Postured among the stolid falconers
(But lobbed his purses to the lutanists),
And, as the eldest son, was first in all
Exercises of eye, mouth, hand and loins.

Then mildew broke across the azure hangings,
Mould on his leather; his horse declined to stir
For all he made it bleed, and his men had time
To jeer at him before the fire took them.
Now, shaven head abased, sandalled feet slow,
He roams the crumbled courts and speaks to none;
But all crave blessing from his hand that clasps
A book, who never feared its pretty sword.

What a shame that a regal house must founder,
Its menials die, its favourites undergo
Unheard-of rape, to emphasise a contrast,
To point one thing out to one person;
Especially since the person could have seen
What it was all about by not laughing
After his father's joke—watching instead,
By changing places with his groom,
    By sixty seconds' thought.

# The Sources of the Past

A broken flower-stem, a broken vase,
    A matchbox torn in two and thrown
Among the scraps of glass:
    At a last meeting, these alone
Record its ruptures, bound its violence,
    And make a specious promise to retain
This charted look of permanence
    In the first moment's pain.

But now the door slams, the steps retreat;
    Into one softness night will blur
The diverse, the hard street;
    And memory will soon prefer
That polished set of symbols, glass and rose
    (By slight revision), to the real mess
Of stumbling, arguing, yells, blows:
    To real distress.

All fragments of the past, near and far,
    Come down to us framed in a calm
No contemplations jar;
    But they grub it up from lapse of time,
And, could we strip that bland order away,
    What vulgar agitation would be shown:
What aimless hauntings behind clay,
    What fussing behind stone?

# The Triumph of Life

When Uncle Pandar Drink pulls down the blinds,
All sequence falters: life, the moving reel,
No longer smoothly, constantly unwinds,

But jerks from still to still. So, we reveal
(Watching no others' poses but our own)
What sober alcohols make us conceal;

Not what we show, but that it shall be shown,
Is all we care about at this first stage,
And that's the time to leave the stuff alone.

Later, we pose with purpose, try to gauge
The look of halted bodies, faces, eyes,
Scissored and pasted on our album-page.

Robbed of its cause and motive, nothing dies.
The darling moment, asked like this, will stay.
—Some time the cogs must mesh, we realise,

The figures move again. But what they say
And how they look no longer matters much:
People get up and dress and go away,

But photographs will never leave our touch.

# The Triumph of Time

When Party-Member Lech lifts up his knout,
We know that's funny and unfunny;
When he gives you a clout,

That's funny, your friends agree,
But for you the joke falls flat.
(Now love's different, do you see.)

We can, we must, we will put up with that:
A man can't go on laughing all the time,
Or minding being laughed at,

And, far from being mere slime or grime,
This is the origin, I propound,
Of our ideas concerning the sublime.

That's fair; but will it still be, when we're found
Fustily grinning at a leg-show,
Funny and unfunny the other way round?

# Here is Where

*Here, where the ragged water*
*Is twilled and spun over*
*Pebbles backed like beetles,*
*Bright as beer-bottles*
*Bits of it like snow beaten,*
*Or milk boiling in saucepan . . .*

Going well so far, eh?
But soon, I'm sorry to say,
The here-where recipe
Will have to intrude its *I*,
Its main verb *want*,
Its *this* at some tangent.

What has this subject
Got to do with that object?
Why drag in
All that water and stone?
Scream the place down *here*,
There's nobody *there*.

The country, to townies,
Is hardly more than nice,
A window-box, pretty
When the afternoon's empty;
When a visitor waits,
The window shuts.

# The Two Purses

A satin purse, devoutly lined
With silk shot many ways, and crammed
Full of mirror, pencil, puff,
Its outside monogrammed,
Within as personally signed
By paper money, smooth and smart:

Such at least would be gift enough,
Device of a rich heart;
—These coins, worn thin, of dull
Metal, this purse of slack wool:
Can you use up this gift of love
And yet find it as durable?

# Nocturne

Under the winter street-lamps, near the bus-stop,
Two people with nowhere to go fondle each other,
Writhe slowly in the entrance to a shop.
In the intervals of watching them, a sailor
Yaws about with an empty beer-flagon,
Looking for something good to smash it on.

*Mere animals:* on this the Watch Committee
And myself seem likely to agree;
But all this fumbling about, this wasteful
Voiding of sweat and breath—is that *animal*?

Nothing so sure and economical.

These keep the image of another creature
In crippled versions, cocky, drab and stewed;
What beast holds off its paw to gesture,
Or gropes towards being understood?

# Act of Kindness

To really give the really valuable,
Or offer the last cigarette,
When shops are shut, to the ungrateful,
Or praise our betters—wishing, we forget

That anything we own is nearly cash,
And to have less of it is dead loss,
That unshared cigarettes are smoke and ash,
That praise is gross.

Not giving should be not living; how to live,
How to deal with any wish to give
When the gift gets stuck to the fingers?
We give nothing we have,
So smiling at strangers

Best suits our book—they cannot tell
Our own from others' words; generous
With common property we seem amiable;
Not to draw a knife
Looks like an act of kindness,
And is, acted to the life.

# Aiming at a Million

And one sort is always trying
To be champion darling,
Bush giant, forest king.

Assorted dryads, gentle,
Raving or doped, shall straddle
That god-almighty bole.

It can no more be the biggest
Than one leaf in a forest
Can dwarf or dry the rest,

And the biggest beauty
Is almost ugly,
Is, or soon will be,

Fleshy and animal,
Or hard and metal.
Then should it stay small?

None outgrows dying,
But height is the end of growing.
A lot is better than nothing.

# Fair Shares for All

A nude steak posing behind gauze
Wins only gastropaths' applause.

An appetite that can be teased
Must be an appetite diseased.

This diagnosis may have point
When love's delivered with the joint.

# To Eros

If only we could throw you away,
Garotte you, weight you, sink you in the bay,
  We could start living, we say.

  Our girls would all relapse
Back into girls—not all that bright, perhaps,
  But ever such decent chaps,

  And when we took them out
To the Sea View, "Doris" we'd hear them shout,
  "Six pints, please, and a milk stout."

  Should we have the sense to go on
Our labour chief, our thick-lipped roarer gone?
  Or should we re-enter upon

  That boring welter of blue,
And at last clear off, not to get shot of you,
  As heroes used to do,

  But parching, fed at the oars,
To net some brute with gape and glare like yours
  And bundle it to these shores?

# Album-Leaf

A photograph can't speak or move its face,
And so the ones we find in frames and books
Seem like the real faces of you and me
Now we no longer like each other's looks;
Self-regard cramps them to stupidity;
Their history of movement leaves no trace.

And this is scarcely queer, but it was queer
That once, during a well-composed embrace,
Something disturbed that studio veneer;
The self-regard of each got holed right through,
Or else we wished it had, or seemed to.

# Ode to the East-North-East-by-East Wind

You rush to greet me at the corner like
   A cheery chap I can't avoid,
And blow my hair into one leaning spike
   To show you're never unemployed.
You sweating, empty-handed labourer,
You bloody-rowelled, mailless courier,
   Before you rush off somewhere new,
      Just tell us what you do.

We know, of course, you blow the windmills
            round,
   And that's a splendid thing to do;
Sometimes you pump up water from the ground;
   Why, darling, that's just fine of you!
And round Mount Everest—such fun!—you blow
Gigantic bits of rock about, for no
   Reason—but every little boy
      Must have his little toy.

The old map-makers must have known you well
   (Punch-drunk sea-captains put them wise)
To draw you with an infant's cheeks that swell
   So that they shut your puffy eyes;
No need for you to care or notice where
You kick and writhe and scream in wincing air,
   Telling the void of your distress,
      Raving at emptiness.

Well now, since blowing things apart's your
        scheme,
    The crying child your metaphor,
Poetic egotists make you their theme,
    Finding in you their hatred for
A world that will not mirror their desire.
Silly yourself, you flatter and inspire
    Some of the silliest of us.
        And is that worth the fuss?

# A Bookshop Idyll

Between the GARDENING and the COOKERY
    Comes the brief POETRY shelf;
By the Nonesuch Donne, a thin anthology
    Offers itself.

Critical, and with nothing else to do,
    I scan the Contents page,
Relieved to find the names are mostly new;
    No one my age.

Like all strangers, they divide by sex:
    *Landscape near Parma*
Interests a man, so does *The Double Vortex*,
    So does *Rilke and Buddha*.

"I travel, you see", "I think" and "I can read"
    These titles seem to say;
But *I Remember You, Love is my Creed*,
    *Poem for J.*,

The ladies' choice, discountenance my patter
    For several seconds;
From somewhere in this (as in any) matter
    A moral beckons.

Should poets bicycle-pump the human heart
    Or squash it flat?
Man's love is of man's life a thing apart;
    Girls aren't like that.

We men have got love well weighed up; our stuff
    Can get by without it.
Women don't seem to think that's good enough;
    They write about it,

And the awful way their poems lay them open
    Just doesn't strike them.
Women are really much nicer than men:
    No wonder we like them.

Deciding this, we can forget those times
    We sat up half the night
Chockfull of love, crammed with bright thoughts,
        names, rhymes,
    And couldn't write.

# Creeper

Shaving this morning, I look out of the window
In expectation: will another small
Tendril of ivy, dry and straw-yellow,
Have put its thin clasp on the garden wall?

Oh dear no. A few arid strands, a few
Curled-up leaves, are all that's left of it.
The children pulled it up for something to do.
My mouth sets in its usual post-box slit.

Fled is that vision of a bottle-green
Fur-coat of foliage muffling the pale brick,
Stamping into the flat suburban scene
A proof of beauty, lovable exotic.

Of course, I know ivy will sweetly plump
Itself all over, shyly barge into crannies,
Pull down lump after elegiac lump,
Then tastefully screen ruin from our eyes.

Then it would all become a legal quibble:
Whose what has wrecked what how and by whose
    what;
And moral: is turning stout wall to rubble
A fool's trick in fact, but not in thought?

We should be thankful to be spared all that
When bank-clerk longings get a short answer,
When someone snatches off our silly hat
And drop-kicks it under a steamroller.

# Gulls

A dozen gulls from the seashore
Across the road swim on a pool
Of rain spilt on the meadow's floor,

And, being off-white, rearrange
Meadow as barnyard, pool as pond,
Themselves as ducks; and this exchange

At first seems meant to entertain,
Merely to fool, or criticise
The sort to whom rain must be rain,

Gulls gulls; or is this hinted at:
No fake is fake—there is no *this*
Less this just for not being *that*?

# A Pill for the Impressionable

Derelict sheds seen from the train,
Standing for nothing in the rain,
Walls lying prone in heaps of stone,

Cold hearths where weeds can barely live,
Quote to the passing sensitive
Banal and clear: *Something died here*.

And something dead invites his tears
Until, miles later, there appears
A graveyard scene in white and green.

In contrast, this looks quite all right;
Smooth turf, rolled paths, well–chosen site:
Everything there in good repair.

If deserts are a larger death,
Why should the traveller catch his breath
When the old ticker gives a kick?

London could die beside the track
To palliate this heart-attack.
The tears we feign are inhumane.

# They Only Move

They only move who travel far,
So whisk me off down roads unsigned
And take me where the good times are.

Whizz past the dance-hall and the bar;
All muffled contact must be blind.
They only move who travel far.

Bortsch, pâté, filthy caviare,
Say I've respectfully declined,
And take me where the good times are.

The social round—Martell, cigar,
Talk about talk—is social grind;
They only move who travel far.

Install me dozing in the car,
Wined, dined, but still unconcubined,
And take me where the good times are.

Lush pastures of the cinema
Will be demanded, once defined.
They only move who travel far.

Fear-indigestion, guilt-catarrh—
If these exist, leave them behind
And take me where the good times are.

Tell me, will movement make or mar?
Then root my body, tell my mind
They only move, who travel far
And take me where the good times are.

# A Note on Wyatt

See her come bearing down, a tidy craft!
Gaily her topsails bulge, her sidelights burn!
There's jigging in her rigging fore and aft,
And beauty's self, not name, limned on her stern.

See at her head the Jolly Roger flutters!
"God, is she fully manned? If she's one short . . ."
Cadet, bargee, longshoreman, shellback mutters;
*Drowned is reason that should me comfort.*

But habit, like a cork, rides the dark flood,
And, like a cork, keeps her in walls of glass;
Cold legacies of brine tingle my blood,
The tide-wind's bated stirrings, as I pass.

Now, jolly ship, sign on a jolly crew:
God bless you, dear, and all who sail in you.

# The Garden

Snuffing the scented afterglow
In summer gardens years ago,
   We tried to conjure there
   A person out of air.

Memory, mixing near with far,
Fabricates links where no links are:
   Perhaps, we now contrive,
   A person did arrive.

Bearings on moving points are bound
To give no sequence but a round;
   We measure and collate,
   But cannot put it straight,

And relish roses at the hour
That might have held that cryptic power,
   Half-asking what it meant,
   Half-granting half-assent.

Wanting to yield, yet just too old,
And just too young quite to withhold,
   We pick the middle way:
   *You ask me first*, we say.

From thinned or trembling lips we hear
Only what makes us wince or sneer:
   *Yes*, the response inane,
   Or *No*, the inhumane.

Debunking what our hearts adore,
Rebunking what our brains abhor,
   Indoors we now adjourn.
   Inward at last we turn.

Our mirror shows one loving face
Pleased to inhabit a blank space.
   To plead *I'm all alone*
   We should be on our own.

# The Voice of Authority:
## A Language Game

Do this. Don't move. O'Grady says do this,
You get a move on, see, do what I say.
Look lively when I say O'Grady says.

Say this. Shut up. O'Grady says say this,
You talk fast without thinking what to say.
What goes is what I say O'Grady says.

Or rather let me put the point like this:
O'Grady says what goes is what I say
O'Grady says; that's what O'Grady says.

By substituting you can shorten this,
Since any god you like will do to say
The things you like, that's what O'Grady says.

The harm lies not in that, but in that this
Progression's first and last terms are I say
O'Grady says, not just O'Grady says.

Yet it's O'Grady must be out of this
Before what we say goes, not what we say
O'Grady says. Or so O'Grady says.

# Mightier than the Pen

Jerking and twitching as he walks,
Neighing and hooting as he talks,
The shabby pundit's prototype,
Smoking his horrible black pipe,
*Balbus* keeps making me feel ill.
I've heard that art's a kind of pill
To purge your feelings, so I'll try
And catch him in my camera's eye,
Transcribe him down to the last hair,
Ambered, though neither rich nor rare.

But will my interests be served
By having such a sod preserved?
Is art much better than a drug,
To cure the man but spare the bug?
And, gentle reader, why should you
Be led vicariously to spew?
Cameras just click, and a click's not
The sound of an effective shot;
Fussing with flash and tripod's fun,
But bang's the way to get things done.

# Autobiographical Fragment

When I lived down in Devonshire
   The callers at my cottage
Were Constant Angst, the art critic,
   And old Major Courage.

Angst always brought me something nice
   To get in my good graces:
A quilt, a roll of cotton-wool,
   A pair of dark glasses.

He tore up all my unpaid bills,
   Went and got my slippers,
Took the telephone off its hook
   And bolted up the shutters.

We smoked and chatted by the fire,
   Sometimes just nodding;
His charming presence made it right
   To sit and do nothing.

But then—those awful afternoons
   I walked out with the Major!
I ran up hills, down streams, through briars;
   It was sheer blue murder.

Trim in his boots, riding-breeches
   And threadbare Norfolk jacket,
He watched me, frowning, bawled commands
   To work hard and enjoy it.

I asked him once why I was there,
    Except to get all dirty;
He tugged his grey moustache and snapped:
    "Young man, it's your duty."

What duty's served by pointless, mad
    Climbing and crawling?
I tell you, I was thankful when
    The old bore stopped calling.

# A Song of Experience

A quiet start: the tavern, our small party,
    A dark-eyed traveller drinking on his own;
We asked him over when the talk turned hearty,
    And let him tell of women he had known.

He tried all colours, white and black and coffee;
    Though quite a few were chary, more were bold;
Some took it like the Host, some like a toffee;
    The two or three who wept were soon consoled.

For seven long years his fancies were tormented
    By one he often wheedled, but in vain;
At last, oh Christ in heaven, she consented,
    And the next day he journeyed on again.

The inaccessible he laid a hand on,
    The heated he refreshed, the cold he warmed.
What Blake presaged, what Lawrence took a stand
    on,
    What Yeats locked up in fable, he performed.

And so he knew, where we can only fumble,
    Wildly in daydreams, vulgarly in art;
Miles past the point where all illusions crumble
    He found the female and the human heart.

Then love was velvet on a hand of iron
    That wrenched the panting lover from his aim;
Lion rose up as lamb and lamb as lion,
    Nausicaa and Circe were the same.

What counter-images, what cold abstraction
    Could start to quench that living element,
The flash of prophecy, the glare of action?
    —He drained his liquor, paid his score and went.

I saw him, brisk in May, in Juliet's weather,
    Hitch up the trousers of his long-tailed suit,
Polish his windscreen with a chamois-leather,
    And stow his case of samples in the boot.

# The English Novel, 1740-1820

The open road winds down from Wilson's farm
To neat lawns and a gilt-edged paradise
Where Pamela walks out on Darcy's arm,
And Fanny Goodwill bobs to Fanny Price.

# Romance

The sound of saxophones, like farmhouse cream,
And long skirts and fair heads in a soft gleam,
Both scale and are the forest-fence of dream.

Picture a youngster in the lonely night
Who finds a stepping-stone from dark to bright,
An undrawn curtain and an arm of light.

Here was an image nothing could dispel:
Adulthood's high romantic citadel,
The Tudor Ballroom of the Grand Hotel.

Those other dreams, those freedoms lost their
   charm,
Those twilight lakes reflecting pine or palm,
Those skies were merely large and wrongly calm.

What then but weakness turns the heart again
Out in that lonely night beyond the pane
With images and truths of wind and rain?

# An Ever-Fixed Mark

Years ago, at a private school
Run on traditional lines,
One fellow used to perform
Prodigious feats in the dorm;
His quite undevious designs
Found many a willing tool.

On the rugger field, in the gym,
Buck marked down at his leisure
The likeliest bits of stuff;
The notion, familiar enough,
Of 'using somebody for pleasure'
Seemed handy and harmless to him.

But another chap was above
The diversions of such a lout;
Seven years in the place
And he never got to first base
With the kid he followed about:
What interested Ralph was love.

He did the whole thing in style—
Letters three times a week,
Sonnet-sequences, Sunday walks;
Then, during one of their talks,
The youngster caressed his cheek,
And that made it all worth while.

These days, for a quid pro quo,
Ralph's chum does what, and with which;
Buck's playmates, family men,
Eye a Boy Scout now and then.
Sex is a momentary itch,
Love never lets you go.

# Out-Patient

Can you stand sanity, committee virtue,
Married, seeing its way, good-humoured
And humouring, over forty
Thank God, enough to drive you mad,

Or insanity with its Look at me
While I do my thing to you or I give up?
Right then, mine's a lobotomy.

Please, there are no midways;
Visit either, like the other.

Change is for kids.

# A Tribute to the Founder

By bluster, graft, and doing people down,
Sam Baines got rich, but, mellowing at last,
Felt that by giving something to the town
He might repair the evils of his past.

His hope was to prevent the local youth
From making the mistakes that he had made:
Choosing expediency instead of truth,
And quitting what was honest for what paid.

A university seemed just the thing,
And that old stately home the very place.
Sam wept with pleasure at its opening.
He died too soon to weep at its disgrace.

Graft is refined among the tea and scones,
Bluster (new style) invokes the public good,
And doing-down gets done in pious tones
Sam often tried to learn, but never could.

# After Goliath

*What shall be done to the man*
*that killeth this Philistine?*
1 Sam. xvii, 27

The first shot out of that sling
Was enough to finish the thing:
The champion laid out cold
Before half the programmes were sold.
And then, what howls of dismay
From his fans in their dense array:
From aldermen, adjutants, aunts,
Administrators of grants,
Assurance-men, auctioneers,
Advisers about careers,
And advertisers, of course,
Plus the obvious b——s in force:
The whole reprehensible throng
Ten times an alphabet strong.
But such an auspicious debut
Was a little too good to be true,
Our victor sensed; the applause
From those who supported his cause
Sounded shrill and excessive now,
And who were they, anyhow?
Academics, actors who lecture,
Apostles of architecture,
Ancient-gods-of-the-abdomen men,
Angst-pushers, adherents of Zen,
Alastors, Austenites, A-test
Abolishers—even the straightest
Of issues looks pretty oblique
When a movement turns into a clique,
The conqueror mused, as he stopped
By the sword his opponent had dropped:
Trophy, or means of attack
On the rapturous crowds at his back?

He shrugged and left it, resigned
To a new battle, fought in the mind,
For faith that his quarrel was just,
That the right man lay in the dust.

# Sight Unseen

As I was waiting for the bus
  A girl came up the street,
Detectable as double-plus
  At seven hundred feet.

Her head was high, her step was free,
  Her face a lyric blur;
Her waist was narrow, I could see,
  But not the rest of her.

At fifty feet I watched her stop,
  Bite at a glove, then veer
Aside into some pointless shop,
  Never to reappear.

This happens every bloody day:
  They about-turn, they duck
Into their car and drive away,
  They hide behind a truck.

Look, if they knew me, well and good,
  There might be cause to run;
Or even saw me—understood;
  No. Not a peep. Not one.

Love at first sight—by this we mean
  A stellar entrant thrown
Clear on the psyche's radar-screen,
  Recognized before known.

All right: things work the opposite
  Way with the poles reversed;
It's galling, though, when girls omit
  To switch the set on first.

# Nothing to Fear

All fixed: early arrival at the flat
Lent by a friend, whose note says *Lucky sod*;
Drinks on the tray; the cover-story pat
And quite uncheckable; her husband off
Somewhere with all the kids till six o'clock
(Which ought to be quite long enough);
And all worth while: face really beautiful,
Good legs and hips, and as for breasts—my God.
What about guilt, compunction and such stuff?
I've had my fill of all that cock;
It'll wear off, as usual.

Yes, all fixed. Then why this slight trembling,
Dry mouth, quick pulse-rate, sweaty hands,
As though she were the first? No, not impatience,
Nor fear of failure, thank you, Jack.
Beauty, they tell me, is a dangerous thing,
Whose touch will burn, but I'm asbestos, see?
All worth while—it's a dead coincidence
That sitting here, a bag of glands
Tuned up to concert pitch, I seem to sense
A different style of caller at my back,
As cold as ice, but just as set on me.

# Toys

A rattle, a woollen ball,
A cuddly animal
Are expendable.
A flameproof nightdress
(5–7 years)
Is pretty. Water-colours
And painting-book will
Keep someone out of trouble
And not make much mess.

Across the aisle are tiers
Of stuff we use on others
As soon as we can: men's
Two-tone cardigans;
Earrings; rings; pens.

# Souvenirs

Photographs are dispensable.
The living, the still young,
Demand no such memorial.

Accusing letters still accuse,
Like the non-accusing.
No harm to be rid of those.

The mind will take surgery.
Though drink, resentment, self-
Defence impair the memory,

Something remains to be cut out.
God, car accident, stroke
Must do to remove it,

For the body adjoins the limb.
Who, heart back to normal,
Could himself cut off his own arm?

# A Point of Logic

Love is a finding-out:
Our walk to the bedroom
(Hand in hand, eye to eye)
Up a stair of marble
Or decently scrubbed boards,
As much as what we do
In our abandonment,
Teaches us who we are
And what we are, and what
Life itself is.

Therefore put out the light,
Lurch to the bare attic
Over buckets of waste
And labouring bodies;
Leave the door wide open
And fall on each other,
Clothes barely wrenched aside;
Stay only a minute,
Depart separately,
And use no names.

# On a Portrait of
# Mme Rimsky-Korsakov

Serene, not as a prize for conflict won,
But mark of never having had to fight,
Needing no mind, because too beautiful,
She sat embodying her unconcern
For all charades of love or symbolism.
  Nicholas was inspecting a brass band,
  Driving to lunch with Borodin and Cui,
  Checking the full score of *The Snow Maiden*.

That dateless look, impersonal above
The coarse placing of the heart's Hollywood,
Writes off poor Janey Morris as a paddler
In joy and agony, a pop-eyed clown
Skinny and thick-lipped with her pomegranate.
  *The Snow Maiden* and the rest of the stuff
  Attain the permanence of print, wax, and
  Footnotes in treatises on orchestration.

# A Chromatic Passing-Note

'That slimy tune' I said, and got a laugh,
In the middle of old Franck's D minor thing:
The dotted-rhythm clarinet motif.

Not always slimy. I thought, at fifteen,
It went to show that real love was found
At the far end of the right country lane.

I thought that, like Keats and the rest of them,
Old Franck was giving me a preview of
The world, action in art, a paradigm.

Yes, I know better now, or different.
Not image: buffer only, syrup, crutch.
'Slimy' was a snarl of disappointment.

# Science Fiction

What makes us rove that starlit corridor
May be the impulse to meet face to face
Our vice and folly shaped into a thing,
And so at last ourselves; what lures us there
Is simpler versions of disaster:           ·
A web that shuffles time and space,
A sentence to perpetual journeying,
A world of ocean without shore,
And simplest, flapping down the poisoned air,
A ten-clawed monster.

In him, perhaps, we see the general ogre
Who rode our ancestors to nightmare,
And in his habitat their maps of hell.
But climates and geographies soon change,
Spawning mutations none can quell
With silver sword or thaumaturge's ring
Worse than their sires, of wider range,
And much more durable.

# The Huge Artifice:
## an interim assessment

Enough of this great work has now appeared
For sightings to be taken, the ground cleared,
Though the main purpose—*what it's all about*
In the thematic sense—remains in doubt.
We can be certain, even at this stage,
That seriousness adequate to engage
Our deepest critical concern is not
To be found here. First: what there is of plot
Is thin, repetitive, leaning far too much
On casual meetings, parties, fights and such,
With that excessive use of coincidence
Which betrays authorial inexperience.
We note, besides these evident signs of haste,
A great deal in most questionable taste:
Too many sex-scenes, far too many coarse
Jokes, most of which have long lost all their force.

It might be felt that, after a slow start,
Abundant incident made amends for art,
But the work's 'greatness' is no more than size,
While the shaping mind, and all that that implies,
Is on a trivial scale, as can be guessed
From the brash nature of the views expressed
By a figure in an early episode, who
Was clearly introduced in order to
Act as some kind of author-surrogate,
Then hastily killed off—an unfortunate
Bid to retrieve a grave strategic lapse.

More damaging than any of this, the gaps
In sensitivity displayed are vast.
Concepts that have not often been surpassed
For ignorance or downright nastiness—
That the habit of indifference is less
Destructive than the embrace of love, that crimes
Are paid for never or a thousand times,
That the gentle come to grief—all these are forced
Into scenes, dialogue, comment, and endorsed
By the main action, manifesting there
An inhumanity beyond despair.

One final point remains: it has been urged
That a few characters are not quite submerged
In all this rubbish, that they can display
Reason, justice and forethought on their day,
And that this partly exculpates the mind
That was their author. Not at all. We find
Many of these in the history of art
(So this reviewer feels), who stand apart,
Who by no purpose but their own begin
To struggle free from a base origin.

# New Approach Needed

Should you revisit us,
Stay a little longer,
And get to know the place.
Experience hunger,
Madness, disease and war.
You heard about them, true,
The last time you came here;
It's different having them.
And what about a go
At love, marriage, children?
All good, but bringing some
Risk of remorse and pain
And fear of an odd sort:
A sort one should, again,
Feel, not just hear about,
To be qualified as
A human-race expert.
On local life, we trust
The resident witness,
Not the royal tourist.

People have suffered worse
And more durable wrongs
Than you did on that cross
(I know—you won't get me
Up on one of those things),
Without sure prospect of
Ascending good as new
On the third day, without
'I die, but man shall live'
As a nice cheering thought.

So, next time, come off it,
And get some service in,
Jack, long before you start
Laying down the old law:
If you still want to then.
Tell your dad that from me.

# Larger Truth

Round Fforestfach, Llansamlet and elsewhere
Some people, it being half past five,
Are going home from work, or whatever they do,
    Or wherever they live.

Others work at night, or are still working
At more different things than I could name,
Or work further away; wherever I stood
    I wouldn't see any of them.

It takes a novelist to say In Swansea
[Let's see the large-scale map] people [all right]
Were [as one man?] packing up work [one kind?]
    And going home [one street?].

Don't plead it's shorthand: he's not done yet.
He sardine-tins us but he plots too,
Merrily tabulating what we're up to,
    And what we think we're up to.

(That is our *donnée*, as it were, *mon bon*,
Our art's vast pattern-from-chaos complex—
Latent meaning exposed as it must be
    By a few swift strokes.)

It takes a poet to be more dishonest,
To pick stuff like this for his harangue,
To pretend that finding or withholding meaning
    Means anything.

# Fiction

Today's last pensioner
Read to and washed up for,
The latest arrival
Weighed and pronounced bonny,
Nurse Lee, her broad shoulders
Trustworthiness itself,
Cycles into the dusk
Thinking of her teapot
And its comfort and cheer—
Adcock's No.1 Brew
(Now only 2/8).

With this rubbed in, we go
Back to 'Gun Law' Part 3,
Where Eli Crumpacker,
A slug through his left arm,
Sways off in the saddle
To rouse the local slobs
Against Sheriff Billings,
And fix to have him shot
Right there in the court-house.
Eli's real poison, but
We know he won't get far.

They—this chap and Nurse Lee—
Are pretty nicely off:
She not scratching gnat-bites,
He with his rent paid up.
Lear just did what Lear did.
Fiction, where that is that
And will stay that, leaves me
Back here again, jealous
To see sorts of people
That feel their there and then,
That move from thing to thing.

# L'Invitation au Voyage

—Welcome aboard the *Nautilus*, monsieur!
I vow you shall confess yourself amazed
Ten thousand times before our cruise is done.
What spectacles are mustered in the deep!
Beauty mere words are useless to depict,
Marvels unknown to science—dangers too,
Which we expunge with electricity.
Salute your comrades now: Ned Land, Conseil,
Brave fellows, and Professor Aronnax,
The eminent pelagiologist,
Whose fund of knowledge is at your desire,
As is my library, well-stocked and calm,
Matchless for the conducting of research.
Should you set store by music, you will find
That organ a trustworthy instrument,
While, for comestibles, we pride ourselves
On our sea-urchin loaf and shark ragout.
    Till dinner, then . . .


—Thanks, Captain Nemo, this is always what
I think I want. But after weeks of Ned
On whaling, good Conseil just being good,
And Aronnax as Aronnax, I might
Start to browse round that matchless library,
Thrum at the organ, savour the thick film
Choking my tongue; and if, one afternoon,
A mermaid swam from the dead coral-groves
And looked in, sea-eyed, at the fat window,
Her olive hair writhing about her head,
Her turquoise nipples pried at by small fish,
Someone like me would say: 'Remarkable!

Behold, my friends, a rare phenomenon!
Doubtless, the lungs have been replaced by gills,
The hide, withstanding eighty atmospheres,
Moreover toughened—the Creator's hand
Lavish as always with new wonderment!'
    The long-boat, please . . .

# Coming of Age

Twenty years ago he slipped into town,
A spiritual secret agent; took
Rooms right in the cathedral close; wrote down
Verbatim all their direst idioms;
Made phonetic transcripts in his black book;
Mimicked their dress, their gestures as they sat
Chaffering and chaffing in the Grand Hotel;
Infiltrated their glass-and-plastic homes,
Watched from the inside; then—his deadliest
    blow—
Went and married one of them (what about that?);
At the first christening played his part so well
That he started living it from then on,
His trick of camouflage no longer a trick.
Isn't it the spy's rarest triumph to grow
Indistinguishable from the spied upon,
The stick insect's to become a stick?

# A.E.H.

Flame the westward skies adorning
Leaves no like on holt or hill;
Sounds of battle joined at morning
Wane and wander and are still.

Past the standards rent and muddied,
Past the careless heaps of slain,
Stalks a redcoat who, unbloodied,
Weeps with fury, not from pain.

Wounded lads, when to renew them
Death and surgeons cross the shade,
Still their cries, hug darkness to them;
All at last in sleep are laid.

All save one, who nightlong curses
Wounds imagined more than seen,
Who in level tones rehearses
What the fact of wounds must mean.

# Oligodora

Open the casket
And accept these gifts,
All I can offer:
A small silver coin
Rubbed smooth by handling,
An unwrapped half-ounce
Of dust and gold–dust,
An emerald, flawed.

This is too little?
Am I in default,
Or are you grasping?
Which of us shows more
Inadequacy?

# Green Heart

Cromyomancy* carves out a preview
And a foretaste of you:
Brittle as gold-leaf the outer skin,
Firmness within;
Full savour, more piercing than any
Peach or strawberry;
The heart will grow.

From the beginning, tears flow,
But of no rage or grief:
Wise cromyomancers know
Weeping augurs belief.

* Divination by means of onions.

# Waking Beauty

Finding you was easy.
At each machete-stroke
The briers—neatly tagged
By Freud the gardener—
Fell apart like cut yarn.
Your door was unfastened.
You awoke instantly,
Returning that first kiss
As in no mere fable.

But how should I get home
Through far thornier tracts
Of the wild rose-jungle,
Dry, aching, encumbered
By a still-drowsy girl?

Your eyes cleared and steadied.
Side by side we advanced
On those glossy giants
And their lattice of barbs:
But they had all withered.

# An Attempt at Time-Travel

Your father had the reins.
He chatted over his shoulder,
Laughing, showing white teeth
Between brown moustache and beard.
His brown bowler was festive.

Next to me, your grandfather,
In a grey suit, clean-shaven,
Smiled a little, watching
The tall horse move. At his fob
A lovely big watch swung.

But you, nine years old
In azure satin blue-trimmed,
Neither turned nor spoke.
At ten, this defeated me.
But at thirty? Twenty?

# In Memoriam W.R.A.
## ob. April 18th, 1963

A *Cricket Match*, between
The *Gentlemen of Cambridge*
And the *Hanover Club*, to be played
By the *Antient Laws* of the *Game*
[Two stumps, no boundaries, lobs,
Single wicket, no pads—all that]
In *Antient Costume*
For a *Good Cause*.

Leading the Gentlemen,
I won the toss and batted.
With a bat like an overgrown spoon
And a racquets ball, runs came fast;
But as, in my ruffles and tights,
I marched to the crease, I was sad
To see you nowhere
About the field.

You would have got the point:
'No boundaries' meant running
Literally each bloody run.
When I 'threw my wicket away'
And, puffing, limped back to my seat,
I wanted to catch your eye
Half-shut with laughter
(And pride and love).

Afterwards, over pints,
Part of a chatting circle,
You would have said I was right
To declare about when I did;

Though the other chaps went for the runs
And got them with plenty in hand,
    What did it matter?
    The game's the thing.

    Later: the two of us:
    'That time—do you remember?—
We watched Wally Hammond at Lord's,
And you said you wished you were him,
And I fixed up a coach, but you said
You were working too hard for exams?
    Oh well. A pity
    You never tried.'

    I know. And I foresee
    (As if this were not fancy)
The on-and-on of your talk,
My gradually formal response
That I could never defend
But never would soften enough,
    Leading to silence,
    And separate ways.

    Forgive me if I have
    To see it as it happened:
Even your pride and your love
Have taken this time to become
Clear, to arouse my love.
I'm sorry you had to die
    To make me sorry
    You're not here now.

# The Evans Country:

## Foreword

There's more to local life today
I know, than what I've found to say;
But when you start recording it
You've got to tone it down a bit.

# Aberdarcy: the Main Square

By the new Boots, a tool-chest with flagpoles
Glued on, and flanges, and a dirty great
Baronial doorway, and things like portholes,
Evans met Mrs Rhys on their first date.

Beau Nash House, that sells Clothes for Gentlemen,
Jacobethan, every beam nailed on tight—
Real wood, though, mind you—was in full view
    when,
Lunching at the Three Lamps, she said all right.

And he dropped her beside the grimy hunk
Of castle, that with luck might one day fall
On to the *Evening Post*, the time they slunk
Back from that lousy week-end in Porthcawl.

The journal of some bunch of architects
Named this the worst town centre they could find;
But how disparage what so well reflects
Permanent tendencies of heart and mind?

All love demands a witness: something 'there'
Which it yet makes part of itself. These two
Might find Carlton House Terrace, St Mark's
    Square,
A bit on the grand side. What about you?

# St Asaph's

A chestnut tree stands in the line of sight
Between the GIRLS entrance and 'Braich-y-Pwll',
Where, half past eightish, Evans shaves his face,
    Squints out the window.

Not that he really wants to get among
Schoolchildren—see, some of the stuff by there,
All bounce and flounce, rates keeping an eye on:
    Forthcoming models.

It's tough, though. Past the winter boughs he'll spot
Bunches of overcoats quite clear; come May,
Just the odd flash of well-filled gingham, and
    Stacks of rich verdure.

You can't win, Dai. Nature's got all the cards.
But bear up: you still know the bloody leaf
From bole or blossom, dancer from the dance.
    Hope for you yet, then.

# Langwell

'Now then, what are you up to, Dai?'
'Having a little bonfire, pet.'
   Bowed down under a sack,
With steps deliberate and sly,
His deacon's face full of regret,
   Evans went out the back.

Where no bugger could overlook
He dumped into a blackened bin
   Sheaves of photogravure,
Now and then an ill-printed book,
Letters in female hands: the thin
   Detritus of amour.

Paraffin-heightened flames made ash
Of *Lorraine Burnet in 3-D*
   And *I'm counting the days*
And *the head girl took off her sash*
And *Naturist* and *can we be*
   *Together for always?*

He piped an eye—only the smoke—
Then left that cooling hecatomb
   And dashed up to his den,
Where the real hot stuff was. A bloke
Can't give any old tripe house-room:
   Style's something else again.

# Pendydd

Love is like butter, Evans mused, and stuck
The last pat on his toast. Breakfast in bed
At the Red Dragon—when Miss Protheroe,
Wearing her weekday suit, had caught the train
Back home, or rather to her place of work,
United Mutual Trust—encouraged thought,
And so did the try-asking-me-then look
The bird who fetched the food had given him.
Scrub that for now. Love is like butter. It
Costs money but, fair play, not all that much,
However hard you go at it there's more,
Though to have nothing else would turn you up
(Like those two fellows on that raft\*, was it?),
Nothing spreads thinner when you're running
    short;
Natural? Well, yes and no. Better than guns,
And—never mind what the heart experts say—
Let's face it, bloody good for you. Dead odd
That two things should turn out so much alike,
He thought, ringing the bell for more of both.

\* Dinghy, actually. Evans is thinking of an episode in *The Bombard Story* (Penguin edition, p. 17).

# Llansili Beach

In his new bather—pretty grand,
Quite frankly—lounging on the sand,
Evans relaxes with the warm
Sun on his back, and studies form.
He lights a fag. Inside a minute
A two-piece with a fair lot in it
Rolls up between him and the sea.
Now watch, and listen, carefully.
He dives straight for his coat, pulls out
His glasses, shoves them on his snout;
Demeanour, casual; gaze, intent.
Years back, he'd have done different:
Whipped off the buggers—anyhow,
Not calmly stuck them on. But now
He stands four-eyed and unashamed,
Also, and here's the point, untamed.
No heartfelt gaze'll satisfy
A real romantic like our Dai;
Wouldn't be natural for a bloke.
He's off: 'Hallo. Care for a smoke?'
Your look/do ratio doesn't change.
All that might is your visual range.

# Brynbwrla

Love's domain, supernal Zion,
    How thy rampart gleams with light,
Beacon to the wayworn pilgrim
    Stoutly faring through the night!

Some, their eyes on heavenly mansions,
    Tread the road their fathers trod,
Others, whom the Foe hath blinded,
    Far asunder stray from God.

And still others—take old Evans—
    Anchor on their jack instead;
Zion, pro- or non- or anti-,
    Never got them out of bed.

Light's abode? There stands the chapel,
    Flat and black against the sky.
Tall hotels ablaze with neon
    Magnetise the sons of Dai.

# Maunders

In the Casino Ballroom,
   The judges disagree
—Some leading local ladies:
   Dai Evans: a J.P.—
On picking Miss Glamorgan
   (West) 1963.

'No, Mr Wynne—on poise, now,
   Miss Clydach just won't do;
And as for, well, her figure,
   It's too . . . too much on view.
Your vote, please, Mr Evans,'
   Smiles Mrs Town Clerk Pugh.

Dai's seen in Clydach's hip-swing,
   Rich bosom and mean face,
Two threats: his own destruction
   By passion's fell embrace,
Or else (a bit more likely)
   Not getting to first base;

Whereas Pugh's time of danger
   Belongs to yesterday,
When choice was more than hedging,
   Reluctance than delay.
—Dai votes against Miss Clydach,
   Then waits his chance to say:

'This show's for youngsters, really.
   The dance'll soon begin,
So why don't you and I, love,
   Pop up the Newlands Inn,
And strengthen our acquaintance
   Over a spot of gin?'

# Fforestfawr

When they saw off Dai Evans's da
The whole thing was done very nice:
Bethesda was packed to the doors,
And the minister, Urien Price,
Addressed them with telling effect.

'Our brother grew rich in respect,'
He told them in accents of fire;
'A man of unshakable strength,
Whom to know was at once to admire.
He did nothing common or mean.'

They'd no notion of coming between
That poor young Dai and his grief,
So each of them just had a word
With him after, well-chosen and brief:
'I looked up to him, boy' sort of touch.

He thanked one and all very much,
But thought, as he waved them goodbye,
Was respect going to be what they felt
When Bethesda did honour to Dai?
No, something more personal, see?

'Hallo, pet. Alone? Good. It's me.
Ah now, who did you think it was?
Well, come down the Bush and find out.
You'll know me easy, because
I'm wearing a black tie, love.'

# Welch Ferry, West Side

The narrow channel where the tankers crawl
And void their cargo into the pipelines,
Encloses, with the railway track that runs
Down to the tinplate works, a chunk of hill,
And here sometimes a pony browses.

Above, on the side farthest from the town,
Beneath the ridge long shorn of pit-prop timber,
A shooting-brake, a 1960 Humber,
Sometimes pulls in among the furze unseen:
Evans is careful with his courting.

Last night, leaving Miss Jones to powder her
Nose in the back, he got out for a stroll,
And noticed—right enough his head was full
Of *oh, you know I do* and *are you sure?*
And *darling, please* and *you're the sweetest*—

That all the smog had lifted, and more stars
Than he knew what to do with filled the sky,
And lighted lighthouse, civic centre, quay,
Chimneys, the pony's pasture, cooling-towers;
'Looks beautiful tonight,' he muttered,

Then raised his voice: 'Eurwen, get moving, do.
You think I want to hang round here all night?
Free over the week-end, are you? I'm not;
I'm boozing with the boys on Saturday,
Sunday's the club . . . All right, then—never.'

# Aldport (Mystery Tour)

Hearing how tourists, dazed with reverence,
Looked through sunglasses at the Parthenon,
Dai thought of that cold night outside the Gents
When he touched Dilys up with his gloves on.

# Aberdarcy: the Chaucer Road

5.40. The Bay View. After the office,
Evans drops in for a quick glass of stout,
Then, by the fruit-machine, runs into Haydn,
Who's marrying the kid he's nuts about.

Of course, he won't pretend it's all been easy:
The wife's three-quarters off her bloody head,
And Gwyneth being younger than their youngest
Leaves certain snags still to be combated.

Oh, no gainsaying that she's quite a handful;
No, not bad-tempered, man, just a bit wild.
He likes a girl to show a touch of spirit;
It's all the better when you're reconciled.

And then, dear dear, what dizzy peaks of passion!
Not only sex, but mind and spirit too,
Like in that thing Prof Hughes took with the
    Honours:
That's right, *The Rainbow*—well, it's all come true.

6.10. The Humber. Evans starts reflecting
How much in life he's never going to know:
All it must mean to really love a woman.
He pulls up sharp outside a bungalow.

6.30. Balls to where. In like a whippet;
A fearsome thrash with Mrs No-holds-barred
(Whose husband's in his surgery till 7);
Back at the wheel 6.50, breathing hard.

7.10. 'Braich-y-Pwll'.—'Hallo now, Megan.
No worse than usual, love. You been all right?
Well, this looks good. And there's a lot on later;
Don't think I'll bother with the club tonight.'

Nice bit of haddock with poached egg, Dundee
    cake,
Buckets of tea, then a light ale or two,
And 'Gunsmoke', 'Danger Man', the Late Night
    Movie—
Who's doing better, then? What about you?

# South

*Where the folks are happy and gay,*
*And the easy way is the right way.*
—OLD SONG

I

A sun as bright as noon in Sicily
Against a soft, crystalline sky,
  Sky-blue mostly.

Bluff, slip-off slope, oxbow lake, meander,
Enormous, and yet like some river
  A long way from here.

Oak and horse-chestnut among half-unknown
Maple, dogwood; the squirrel's kin,
  The crow's cousin.

New wonders, but familiar in the mind,
A world of greenwood without end,
  God's England.

Actual dweller in the golden age,
Exempt from man's glum heritage:
  The noble savage,

At any rate as seen from a distance.
And so, of course, Wordsworth's peasants
  In all innocence,

And, if you like, the men of the Just City,
Fabulously rich without money,
  And, perforce, free.

II

The usual: ranch-style, eat-o-mat, drive-in,
Headlight, tail-light, floodlight, neon,
  And air-pollution—

Except the last, tolerable? Yes,
But, through street after street, the voice
  Of something vicious.

*You blind? Can't you see they're inferior?—*
*Our women's what they're really after—*
  *You got to use fear—*

*If they try it I'm shooting me a coon—*
*Keep 'em out of uptown, midtown—*
  *Keep 'em down.*

Across the tracks, a bit more of the usual:
Mad, hopeless, understandable
  Design to kill.

In the libraries, books about justice,
Freedom, innocence, goodness.
  No use.

III

The history of thought is a side-issue
When events begin, an idea
  Is a lie.

To north and west, hope, not yet in vain;
Mexico too, not an illusion;
  Africa, even;

But in the South, nothing now or ever.
For black and white, no future.
  None. Not here.

# Bobby Bailey

Norbury Avenue. And there's Bobby Bailey's—
    Flagged pathway, tall front door;
What super fun to just turn up, and find him
    Sprawled on the playroom floor,

Toppling West Kents, Carabineers, 5th Lancers
    With a mad marble-barrage,
Doling out Woodbines, Tizer and eclairs in
    The loft above the garage,

Or mouthing *Shitface!* at his sister Janet,
    Vision so rarely seen,
Slightly moustached, contemptuous, fine-featured,
    Full-breasted, and sixteen.

Fun to turn up. But back in '35 they
    Moved to a place called Penn,
And Janet's kids must be, what, twelve years older
    Than she and Bobby then?

Of course. I know that, every year, some people
    Simply get up and go
Too far for you to see, much less drop in on,
    Less yet stay with. I know

"The past" is a good name for what's all over;
    You can't, in fact, return
To what isn't a place. It does sound like an
    Easy lesson to learn.

# Lost

Ghosts of the dead appear
Thus or thus, through a fold in time,
Out of darkness, on one night of the year,
To the wrong man, after some pantomime
With salt, blood, henbane, when the rash thief
Sets foot on the stair, touches the necklace;
All act on large or intricate summonses,
And, seen and heard, compel no belief.

But a living ghost will walk unseen,
At a mere sight or sound, unheard,
Called into motion by an apple-green
Dress, fair hair sun-bleached, a dog's bark,
Ash-buds in a vase, the voices of
Young children running across a park;
Such bodiless presence comes at a word:
Beauty, pain, love.

# Shitty

Look thy last on all things shitty
    While thou'rt at it: soccer stars,
Soccer crowds, bedizened bushheads
    Jerking over their guitars,

German tourists, plastic roses,
    Face of Mao and face of Ché,
Women wearing curtains, blankets,
    Beckett at the ICA,

High-rise blocks and action paintings,
    Sculptures made from wire and lead:
Each of them a sight more lovely
    Than the screens around your bed.

# Lovely

Look thy last on all things lovely
   Every hour, an old shag said,
Meaning they turn lovelier if thou
   Thinkst about soon being dead.

Do they? When that 'soon' means business
   They might lose their eye-appeal,
Go a bit like things unlovely,
   Get upstaged by how you feel.

The best time to see things lovely
   Is in youth's primordial bliss,
Which is also when you rather
   Go for old shags talking piss.

# Peacefully

REGER, Max, German composer
. . . died 11th May, 1916.
The second battle of Verdun had started
Eight days earlier. Once,
My feeling would have been: Poor sod;
Bad enough anyway, of course,
But to be hauled off at that stage,
With friends lost, missing, under fire,
And peace quite unimaginable,
Must have been a good deal harder.

Whereas with old BRUCH, Max
(1838-1920)—
Bad enough anyway, of course,
But to be hauled off any time
After the war, even though
It had turned out against your country,
Must have made it that much easier.

Perhaps. But when AMIS, Kingsley,
Gets his last morning papers
('Shall I take them in to him, then, doctor?'
—'Can't do any harm now, nurse.'),
And sees *Famine in Burma Spreading*,
*Italian Civil War Escalates*,
*Oxford Rebellion: Many Dead*,
I predict something different:

Bloody good! That'll teach 'em!
With luck, a good ten thousand'll
Go before it's my turn—
Most of the bastards younger than me.
Bad enough anyway, of course,
But that tiny sliver of hope
That some fool might drop the bomb
If not today, then next week
(And there's always the sun going nova),
Just might make a bit of difference—

Or at least distraction from picturing the scene
(Maugham, is it? Shaw? One of that lot)
Where a chap looks up from the *Times* and says,
'You saw old Kingsley's gone?'—'Christ!
I hadn't heard he was ill.'—'No age
To speak of, was he?' And the whole crew
Try to conceal their glee that this
Time it still isn't them.
'Bad enough anyway, of course,
But one gathers he dropped off quite peacefully.'

# Three Scenarios:

## I - Reasons

When she was just turned twenty
Anne got run over by a lorry,
   And they had to take her legs off
A good way above the knee.

She refused to be defeated
By it: had herself fitted
   With a pair of artificials.
'Life's what you make it' she said,

And in a year she was skating,
Riding a bike, dancing,
   Like any other youngster
—Except for the one thing.

'That's life. To take on a woman
In my sort of condition'
   She said 'would call for a very
Extraordinary man.'

Then up turned an admirer
Who filled the bill; a charmer
   But serious—in less than
A month he married her.

On the wedding night he unfastened
Those legs of hers; what happened
   Then, well, never mind, but
She was crying before the end

At his awful vile foulness.
'How could you be so heartless?'

126

She said 'and I was thinking
You got me into this

'In spite of, not because of
Me being so much worse off
   Than other girls; through pity
Even, if not love.'

'Sorry if I've shocked you;
I didn't mean to hurt you,
   But legless girls fetch me'
He said 'and you're gorgeous, too.

'And would you sooner settle
For somebody quite normal
   Who had to grit his teeth to
Make it with you at all?

'And the other problem:
A man like that would need some
   Distraction, say. But I can
Get all I want at home.'

She was still indignant,
But after a great argument
   Lasting all night, she
Said she saw what he meant,

And after all, no one,
No one can choose the reason
   (She told herself later)
Why someone else takes them on.

127

## II - Nicely

Mr Robinson was a stockbroker
With a nice house down by the river
Nicely furnished, nice garden,
And a nice wife and nice children.
The business was doing nicely, too,
And he had enough to turn his hand to,
Like golf, bridge, carpentry, boating,
The garden, of course. And yet something
Was not right, was not there;
It all suddenly turned sour,
And at the party for his fiftieth birthday
He realised he would give, well, half his money
For anything in the way of a change of scene
And a clean break from the old routine.

The stage was set for that ring at the bell:
'Chalkie, by God! It's not possible!
Must be thirty years, or nearly,
Since our crowd went through it at Benghazi.
Scotch? Cheers! You must have dinner with us!'
—Later: 'Robbie, my lad, I've a serious
Proposition to put to you. In '44
The Jerries dumped a load of treasure,
Diamonds, works of art, bullion
Worth something like half a million,
Although it's not the cash that counts
But, I don't know what to call it, the romance:
Well, it's in . . . a place I know about;
Will you help me to get it out?'

But that was not what happened. Instead,
Something went wrong with Robinson's inside,
And he was put in a nice nursing-home
With a nice doctor, nice nurses, all of them
Very nice, and is doing quite nicely
Considering, for the moment anyway.
Now and then he notices his change of scene,
And the clean break from his old routine.

## III - Reborn

'Hell' said the Devil, as it might have been,
'Is eternal banishment from God
   And from the whole of his creation.
Your sentence starts now. This is your cell.'

'Even mortal prisoners' I said
'On shorter terms, are allowed more than this
   Featureless box, which excludes me
From man's creation too. Is that entailed?'

The Devil, or whoever it was, said
'I am not a barbarian. This I grant:
   A house literally nowhere,
Solitary confinement, but with things.

'You are denied visitors and pets
And all extrinsic aids, like news or drink;
   But art, man's sole true creation,
I allow in whatever form you choose.'

'I see the house is finite' I said
'And also confined; so books are my choice.'
   'Agreed' he said. 'You will know them
All by heart in a million years or so.'

Returned after some such interval,
'How do you find eternity?' asked
   The Devil, or a similar being.
'Oh, that. All right' I said, and shut my book.

'Take this—most instructive, and about you,
Oddly enough, in more than one role:
   *Paradise Lost*. Of course you know it.'
'And so must you these days. Every word.'

'Not quite. I spent some millennia
Learning how to annul memory—that
   Much-advertised but precarious
Sole weapon of yours—just as I wish,

'And so am free of you and eternity,
And can do more than either of you,
   Who cannot annul a sparrow's footprint
Once it is a fact. May I read on?'

'To hell with you. No books and no house:
Nothing. No things. Just you in the dark.'
   'Not a barbarian? Continue,
While I every moment am reborn.'

# Report

*From*: His Highness the Inspector-General
*To*: Lord Secretary of the Defence Chamber
*Subject*: Pre-training Environment S3

Telepanaesthetic probes in depth
Augment Monitoring Centre records:
The above Environment is the most conduceful
Of all visitationed on our Tour.
Adverse conditions intensity 9
—Physical, psychical and mental—
Leave pre-trainees' morale undecreased,
Even enhanced. With such an affect-pattern,
Nothing in Arcturian capability
Can impedite them in oppugnancy-zones.
(Self-destruct index .07 only.)

*Prescribed*: 1. Soonest mobilisation
(With mindfulness to the state of the war)
Into Commando and Marine units.
2. Creating suppletory Environments,
S3 adhibited as paradigm.

*Note for Linguistic Section*: Subjects
Refer (in their most widespread symbology)
To the duration of their pre-training as 'Life'
And to their Environment as 'Earth'.

# Ode to Me

Fifty today, old lad?
Well, that's not doing so bad:
All those years without
Being really buggered about.
The next fifty won't be so good,
True, but for now—touch wood—
You can eat and booze and the rest of it,
Still get a lot of the best of it,
While the shags with fifty or so
Actual years to go
Will find most of them tougher,
The going a good bit rougher
Within the Soviet sphere—
Which means when the bastards are here,
Making it perfectly clear
That all that double-think
(Both systems on the blink,
East and West the same,
And war just the name of a game)
Is the ballocks it always was.
But will it be clear? Because
After a whole generation
Of phasing out education,
Throwing the past away,
Letting the language decay,
And expanding the general mind
Till it bursts, we might well find
That it wouldn't make much odds
To the poor semi-sentient sods
Shuffling round England then
That they've lost what made them men.

So bloody good luck to you, mate,
That you weren't born too late
For at least a chance of happiness,
Before unchangeable crappiness
Spreads over all the land.
Be glad you're fifty—and
That you got there while things were nice,
In a world worth looking at twice.
So here's wishing you many more years,
But not all that many. Cheers!

# Wasted

That cold winter evening
The fire would not draw,
And the whole family hung
Over the dismal grate
Where rain-soaked logs
Bubbled, hissed and steamed.
Then, when the others had gone
Up to their chilly beds,
And I was ready to go,
The wood began to flame
In clear rose and violet,
Heating the small hearth.

Why should that memory cling
Now the children are all grown up,
And the house—a different house—
Is warm at any season?

# Festival Notebook

CLOSING SCENES of the Salisbury Festival:
Haydn and Mozart in St. Edmund's Church,
A building soon to be deconsecrated
Because irrelevant to civic needs
And turned into a meaningful hotel.
Involuntarily the mind throws up
Fancies of Japanese, back from Stonehenge,
Quaffing keg bitter by the pulpit stair,
Swedes booking coach-tours in the chancel.

SALISBURY becomes a part of Area 5
In 1974, and so its mayor,
Whose office dates back to 1611
(The year of the Authorised Version, actually),
Will soon be as irrelevant as the church,
But need not be turned into anything.

LATER THAT NIGHT, outside the City Hall,
Past the Cadena, Debenham's, Joyland,
Men of the 1st Bn. the Royal Scots
Perform the historic ceremony of Tattoo.
Plaids, bonnets, flash of tenor-drummers' sticks,
The pipes, stir the blood unmeaningfully
Till 'Jesus Christ, Superstar' rings out
In the quick march, and relevance is restored.

# Crisis Song

It's one more glass of unpoisonous wine,
  And one more pint of beer
Made out of stuff like malt and hops:
  Drink it while it's here,
And one more cut off the round of beef—
  You'll be scoffing snoek next year.

See, every wash with a cake of soap
  Means one less without;
And you get a mark for every shave
  Before the steel runs out.
(The same applies to paper reserves:
  You know what I'm on about.)

There's socks that last you a bit and don't
  Make your feet itch and sweat,
Jackets that don't shrink in the rain,
  Shoes that keep out the wet,
All of them actually in the shops
  At the moment—the best point yet.

So it's round the telly as long as it lasts
  And down to the old hi-fi
(But watch it there: no records soon
  With vinyl in short supply);
Christ, even those colour supplements
  Will look beautiful by and by.

Yes, relish the lot, and collar the lot
  In a terminal spending-spree,
But one thing you can forget, because
  Of this firm guarantee:
There's going to be stacks of bloody salt
  —Mined by you and me.

# A Reunion

I

*Dear* Bill, *To confirm—we meet*
*At the Allied Services Club,*
*6 Upper Greenhill Street*
*(Opposite Farringdon Tube),*
*On Friday 11th July*
*Any time after 6 p.m.;*
*Informal—but wear a tie!*
*Yours very sincerely*, Jim.

Thirty years ago
Jim had been Sergeant Woods,
The chap you did well to know
If you wanted some over-the-odds
Bit of kit, travel warrant, repair;
A lot came his way from his friend
The O.C., Major MacClure—
One of those who had 'hoped to attend'.

I hoped so too, on the whole,
As I started off: you could say
That Sandy MacClure was a real
Panjandrum of shits on his day,
But the bugger could get you to laugh:
Killing take-offs of his mates,
The trip-wires he laid for the Staff,
That truck-load of Yank cigarettes.

Jim was a quieter lad,
Ever ready to reminisce
About life in Hyderabad,
And also to take the piss;
A fine bloody pair they were
(My Christ, how they screwed around)

138

To remember so loud and clear,
But others soon came to mind:

Slosher Perkins, disciple of Marx,
With his pamphlets and posters; Burnett
(Was he one of the company clerks?),
The booziest sod of the lot;
Young Taylor, obstreperous enough
In spite of that choirboyish look;
Shy little Corporal Clough,
Who would talk about Shelley and Blake.

And behind them a hundred more
With a background of pay-parades,
The Naafi, the technical store,
Being lectured about grenades,
Guard-mountings, vehicle pools,
Defaulters, inspections of kit
And barrack-rooms, spares and tools,
And gas-capes and God knows what.

Then farmyards and cobbled roads
Full of sun, fresh fruit, village wells,
Tents pitched in the leaf-strewn woods,
Slow crossing of iced-up canals,
Those seasons, that mutable scene
Trodden through in the end—all that,
Plus litres of lager and wine
And a sniff or so at the frat.*

* 'Fraternisation' between Allied troops and German
nationals, including females, was forbidden by order of
General Eisenhower in 1944. Phrases like 'a piece of frat'
soon became current.

## II

Now, up a green-linoed stair,
Past walls in need of a wash
I went, turned a corner, and there
Was Jim, with a grey moustache
And a belly, but still—'Good God!'
I said, 'you look just the same,
You treacherous, miserable sod!'
'I'm sorry,' he said—'what's the name?'

Soon seen to. The place had the look
Of a rather expensive canteen:
Sandwiches, cakes and cake,
Card-tables, a fruit-machine,
A fag-machine and a bar.
This served in effect, I found,
Scotch, gin and tonic, and beer;
You struggled to stand your round.

Oh, one other drink, ginger ale,
Stood before my incredulous eye.
'So what are you up to, Bill?
Tom Burnett. —No, I kissed it good-bye
When my liver went up the creek:
Had to settle for this instead;
You still have the company, like.
—Harry Clough? Nice fellow. He's dead.'

It went on for an hour, about,
To the point where a half-known face
Shoved itself forward to shout,
'This beer's a bloody disgrace,
And you can't even get bloody served!'
Jim coped. The chap who had been
Young Taylor was quite well preserved,
Though his jowls were a little wan.

That was sort of the signal for scoff;
'It shows you how things have changed:
Back then, he'd have had to fuck off
Or get handled,'—Perkins had ranged
His cardboard plate next to mine—
'But you can't really do that now,
And it isn't just auld lang syne;
As if we've grown up, somehow.'

Clifford Perkins (Slosher as was)
Said society's values were more
And more unencumbered, because
No bugger could save the entire
Class structure from final decay.
I waited for Jim to respond
In the old familiar way,
But he nodded and smiled and yawned.

With the coffee and cake and cakes
Came the speeches, which finally squashed
A discussion of heart-attacks;
The first on his feet was sloshed,
And Jim had him off them again,
Quite politely, in five seconds flat.
This would all have been funny then,
I said to myself, or it might.

The second and third and the rest
Stood sober enough and to spare
On things like the lately deceased
And how lucky we were to be there;
I was turning my thoughts to booze
When that side of it came to an end:
Ex-major MacClure—'Cheers, boys!'—
Had realised his hope to attend.

He had changed very little: he wore
Bifocals now, but his face
Was as sharply defined as before,
His hair still abundant; his voice
Was the same semi-muted shout
When he talked, as he did for a while,
Of blokes I knew nothing about;
And, by God, he had kept up his style.

I finally got a word through:
Had he run into Nicholls at all?
(A privilege granted to few
Is meeting a pratt on the scale
Of Nicholls: by common consent
A nitwit not fit to shift shit;
Whether more of a bastard or cunt,
Views varied, one has to admit.)

None who saw it could ever forget
MacClure as he took Nicholls off:
Him bumming your last cigarette,
His frown, then his clangorous laugh,
But now, as I mentioned the name
And a bunch of us stood at the bar,
Sandy announced with aplomb
That they met now and then for a jar.

Disbelief, rather broadly expressed,
Was called for, but not even Jim
Seemed shocked or surprised in the least,
So I said, 'A jar with *him*?
You must be out of your—hey!
I remember you swearing, back then,
They could come and take you away
If you ever drank with him for fun.'

'Oh yes?' said MacClure. 'Well, you know
How it is—you exaggerate. And
It was all a long time ago;
Now we're older, we understand
Other blokes, or some of us do.
One thing about Nicholls, Bill,
He always stuck up for you,
And you needed a spot of goodwill.'

He spoke at his customary pitch,
And with his customary grin.
Not much later, Jim looked at his watch
And mentioned packing it in.
No one suggested a song—
Well, no one still there was tight,
And the lads started getting along
(Bar those booked in for the night).


III

What had brought us together before
Was over, no doubt about that;
What had held us together was more
Than, whether you liked it or not,
Going after a single aim,
One procedure laid down from above;
In their dozens, no two the same,
Small kinds and degrees of love.


144

And that was quite natural then,
When to do what we had to do
Showed us off perfectly, when
We were not so much young as new,
With some shine still on us, unmarked
(At least only mildly frayed),
When everything in us worked,
And no allowances made.

So, when one of us had his leave stopped,
Was awarded a dose of the clap
Or an extra guard, or was dropped
Up to his ears in the crap,
Or felt plain bloody browned off,
He never got left on his own:
The others had muscle enough
To see that he soldiered on.

Disbandment has come to us
As it comes to all who grow old;
Demobilised now, we face
What we faced when we first enrolled.
Stand still in the middle rank!
See you show them a touch of pride!—
Left-right, left-right, bags of swank—
On the one-man pass-out parade.

*All characters and details in this poem are fictitious.*

# Their Oxford

I

To reach the centre you turn left, not right,
And drive halfway to Abingdon before
You start to double back past building-site,
Paella joint, hair-stylist, hi-fi store,

By uncouth alleys to the old hotel,
Now newly faced. Here, thirty years ago,
They tried their gravelled best to do you well;
Floors creaked, the food was flat, the waiters slow,

But parents and fiancées drawled at ease
Here, mad old ladies gibbered freely on,
Dour scholars, warmed by taking their degrees,
Were safe with sherry, while a queerish don

Could lush up his star pupil. Here, today,
Floors creak, the food is glozed, the waiters skive;
You have to do yourself well as you may
In the dimmed bar, where fifty Finns arrive

Just before you, and budding businessmen,
Though dressed like actors, call at bruisers' pitch
For Highland malt with stacks of ice. What then?
You take a stroll up the Cornmarket, which

Is now a precinct (not the sacred sort);
Beyond We're Every-Wear there still exists
The Roebuck, once the unarranged resort
Of hearties, Bodley readers, botanists,

Where men in long top-coats would snort and
    scratch,
Meat-market porters gulp their morning break,
And stall-boys jostle: now, yards off, you catch
The surge and thunder of a discothèque.


II

In my day there were giants on the scene,
Men big enough to be worth laughing at:
Coghill and Bowra, Lewis and Tolkien.
Lost confidence and envy finished that.

A different sense of style was not to seek—
Champagne breakfasts (or were they mythical?),
The OUDS, the Union set, the Playhouse clique—
Its fairest, choicest crown the Commem. Ball.

Do costly girls still throng the chequered lawn,
All bosom and bright hair, as they did then,
And laugh and dance and chatter until dawn
With peacock-minded, donkey-voiced young men?

Where once a line of college barges lay,
Haunt of the rich (comparatively) few,
A single hulk welters and rots away;
So goes that Oxford that I hardly knew.

With mildly coveting what I could see
Went disapproval, but at this remove,
When no one here cares how it used to be
Except the old, can I still disapprove?

What seemed to me so various is all one,
A block of time, which like its likenesses
Looks better now the next such has begun;
Looks, and in this case maybe really is.

# Three Shorts:

## I - Senex

To find his sexual drives had ceased
   For Sophocles was no disaster;
He said he felt like one released
   From service with a cruel master.

I envy him—I miss the lash
   At which I used to snort and snivel;
Oh that its unremitted slash
   Were still what makes me drone and drivel!

## II - Advice to a Story-Teller

*after Martial*

That time you heard the archbishop fart
   You did quite right to say;
And should the ploughboy turn up gold
   The news would make our day;
But when the ploughboy farts henceforth
   Forget about it, eh?

# III - The Shrimp in the Rubbish-Bin

I lived in my own world of sea
   Till someone came and caught me,
Boiled me and sent me to a shop
   Where someone came and bought me.
I ask you, human beings all,
   Was that the way to treat me,
To do to me what you have done
   And then not even eat me?

# Drinking Song

Look at old Morrison!
Isn't he wonderful?
Fit as a fiddle
　　And tight as a tick;
Seventy-seven
And spouting his stories—
Just listen a minute
　　And laugh yourself sick.

Same with the other chaps:
Bloody good company,
Never let anyone
　　Drink on his own;
Out of your parish
Or widowed or derelict—
Once you're in here
　　You're no longer alone.

Different for Weatherby,
Struck with incontinence,
Mute in his wheelchair
　　And ready to go;
Different for Hooper,
Put back on the oxygen,
Breathing, but breathing
　　Uncommonly slow.

Did what we could, of course,
While there was anything;
Best to remember 'em
   Not as they are,
But as they used to be,
Chattering, chaffing and . . .
You go and eat
   And I'll stay in the bar.

# Farewell Blues

Bongo, sitar, 'cello, flute, electric piano, bass guitar,
Training Orchestra, Research Team, Workshop,
 Group, Conservatoire,
*Square Root, Nexus, Barbaresque, Distortions,*
 *Voltage*—bloody row,
For Louis Armstrong, Mildred Bailey, Walter Page
 and Sidney Catlett lie in Brunswick churchyard
 now.

Trumpets gelded, drums contingent, saxophones
 that bleat or bawl,
Keyless, barless, poor-man's Boulez, improvising
 on fuck-all,
Far beyond what feeling, reason, even mother wit
 allow,
While Muggsy Spanier, Floyd O'Brien, Sterling
 Bose and Henry Allen lie in Decca churchyard
 now.

Dead's the note we loved that swelled within us,
 made us gasp and stare,
Simple joy and simple sadness thrashing the
 astounded air;
What replaced them no one asked for, but it turned
 up anyhow,
And Coleman Hawkins, Johnny Hodges, Bessie
 Smith and Pee Wee Russell lie in Okeh church-
 yard now.

# Two Impromptus:

## I - Delivery Guaranteed

Death has got something to be said for it:
There's no need to get out of bed for it;
   Wherever you may be,
   They bring it to you, free.

## II - Equal Made

Only the actions of the just
Smell sweet and blossom in their dust,
Which does the just about as much
Good as a smart kick in the crotch.